Mended

Restore and Rebuild What Was Broken

Dr. Ivon L. Valerie

Sapiential Publishing

CONTENTS

DEDICATION

To every soul who has ever felt the sting of brokenness but chose to pick up the pieces and believe in restoration—this book is for you.

To the silent warriors who mend in the shadows, to the ones who hold on when it's easier to let go, and to those who believe that even shattered things can be made beautiful again—may you find the strength to restore and rebuild.

And to my Faith & Works Ministries family—thank you for being living proof that love can heal and community can restore. I love you.

ACKNOWLEDGEMENTS

Mending is never a solitary act. It takes a community, a family, and a God who specializes in restoration.

First, thank you to my Lord and Savior for being the ultimate restorer who pieces us back together when we feel beyond repair.

To my beautiful family, thank you for your constant love, patience, and unwavering belief in me. You've been my safe place, strength, and reason to keep going.

To the incredible Faith & Works Ministries family, you embody the message of restoration. Your stories, strength, and resilience have inspired every word on these pages.

To Sapiential Publishing House—your excellence in bringing this book to life has been unmatched. Thank you for treating this work with care and vision.

And to every reader—thank you for trusting me with your healing journey. I pray this book is the tool you need to mend what was broken and rebuild something even stronger.

THE TRAUMA DETOX

From the outside, it might look as if healing only requires a single moment of realization—that once you name your trauma, you simply walk away from its grip. But real transformation runs deeper. **The Trauma Detox** trilogy understands that after you face the raw truth of your wounds (*Scarred*), you still need a daily process that untangles old patterns and renews your heart. That's where *Mended* comes in.

This second book isn't about ignoring the scars you've revealed; it's about tending to them, soothing them day by day until they fade from open sores to testimonies of resilience. Think of it like physical therapy after a major injury. You don't just bandage a broken bone and call it done. You practice exercises, gradually rebuild muscle, and steadily regain full use. *Mended* offers the same approach for your soul, mind, and emotional well-being.

1. **Scarred** introduced you to the magnitude of your trauma. It helped you strip away denial, letting the light in so you can see what truly needs healing.

2. **Mended** is about applying faith-grounded, practical steps to

renew your rhythms—your morning routines, late-night anxieties, and how you respond to stress, triggers, and relationships. Think of it as your rehab phase, reinforcing your progress in *Scarred* with tangible, consistent action.

3. **Bloom** will eventually invite you to thrive, not just survive. You'll discover a fresh purpose, a daily joy that defies old sorrow, and the chance to become a beacon for others. But first, we must strengthen and mend what was broken.

By calling this series **The Trauma Detox**, we acknowledge that trauma saturates every corner of your being: your mind replays painful events, your body reacts with tension or panic, and your spirit can feel drained of hope. *Mended* offers the daily acts that gently purge these toxins. It's not a race to see how fast you can "fix" yourself; it's a patient journey where each strategy—grounding techniques, boundary-setting, or adopting new prayer habits—accumulates into lasting change.

As you read *Mended*, expect both encouragement and challenge. You'll be asked to step into routines that might feel foreign initially, but in time, they'll become second nature. Each page invites you to trust that God's restorative power is present in every breath you take, every safe boundary you establish, and every moment of self-compassion you practice. The goal is that by the end, you don't just know you survived trauma; you feel it in your bones that you're mending, day by day, brick by brick, breath by breath.

Now, let's begin this hands-on portion of your healing. Don't worry if it feels intimidating—every big journey starts with small, faithful steps. As you commit to these exercises, keep your eyes on the ultimate promise: that a life beyond woundedness is possible and that *Mended* is the bridge spanning from acknowledging your scars to living renewed with hope.

INTRODUCTION

Imagine waking up in the morning, feeling the gentle rays of sunlight peeking through your window, yet a subtle heaviness still lingers in your chest. You've named the scars and faced down old memories, but your heart still aches to find its rhythm—a steady, peaceful cadence that isn't so easily undone by triggers or fears. You long to move beyond survival mode, to embrace each day with fresh energy and freedom. *Mended* is the next step on that path, a guide to actively weaving together the pieces of your healing so that you live, breathe, and walk differently than before.

If *Scarred* was about naming your pain, *Mended* is about rolling up your sleeves and tending the wound day by day. It's practical work: learning to calm your thoughts when anxiety tries to rule them, re-centering yourself in faith when negative voices whisper discouragement, and gently rebuilding trust in a God who still sees you even when you feel lost. This isn't an insurmountable theory; it's the nuts and bolts of restoring emotional balance, one simple practice at a time.

Perhaps you've wondered, "Will I always feel these flashes of panic? Will I ever sleep soundly without nightmares?" The answer is that healing can grow in the soil that once felt barren but often does so gradually. *Mended* offers small daily steps—prayerful pauses, intentional routines, and faith-based exercises that help loosen the tight grip of trauma. Think of it as a gentle companion walking beside you, showing you how to cultivate calm in anxious moments and reclaim the parts of your life you once believed were gone forever.

Yet, this isn't merely about emotional maintenance. It's about rediscovering the joys you'd left behind, the dreams you've packed away in a box labeled "impossible." It's about reestablishing faith as the glue that holds each newly healed piece together, reminding you that God's power isn't just for grand miracles—it's for the everyday miracle of a calmer morning, a shared laugh without fear in the background, a surge of gratitude that replaces sorrow.

As you turn these pages, I pray you feel a spark of courage whenever you consider the habits and tools here. Maybe you'll try a breathing exercise that anchors you in the present moment or set a boundary that allows your heart to rest instead of bracing for the next blow. These may sound like small efforts, yet each one is a statement of faith—declaring that your life isn't forever chained to trauma's demands.

We'll dive into tangible practices. We'll talk about nurturing your body through gentle movement and discovering the power of spiritual alignment when your mind races with doubts. Most of all, we'll explore how faith becomes a steady anchor in this process, reminding you that you're never without God's help.

Many have walked this road before you. They can testify that while the journey may not be instant or easy, it can lead to profound transformation. Day by day, habit by habit, you'll sense the loosening of trauma's grip and the awakening of a new normal—one less defined by memories of pain and more by moments of laughter, purpose, and genuine rest. The strength you develop along the way becomes a quiet assurance that your future holds more than your past tried to steal.

So, prepare your heart. Approach *Mended* like a sacred invitation. Yes, you may have old triggers or unanswered questions, but those do not disqualify you from healing. Through consistent, grace-filled actions, you'll discover a life rhythm that fortifies you against old fears. Little by little, you'll see that each prayer, each mindful breath, and each faith-anchored decision weaves your fragmented pieces into a network of renewed wholeness.

No matter how fragile or uncertain you feel, trust that God's hand is gently guiding you toward that place of calm waters. Every effort you invest in these pages is a testament to your resolve and His unfailing presence. You're not merely trying to "get over" trauma; you're learning to be *mended* from the inside out, day by faithful day.

Welcome to the next phase of your journey. May *Mended* be the practical, hope-filled companion that shows you how to transform understanding into real, sustained change. And as you step forward with each new day, may your spirit testify, "Yes, I am healing. Yes, I am growing stronger. And yes, with God's help, I am learning to live free."

Proof of Healing

David's Story

I was the guy who always said, "I'm fine." Even as my marriage crumbled, even as I drowned my loneliness in whiskey, even when I lost everything that mattered—I still said, "I'm fine."

Until I wasn't.

I met Apostle Dr. Ivon Valerie when I was on the verge of losing the last thing I had—myself. I didn't want to talk about feelings. I didn't want some "rah-rah, you can do it" pep talk. I wanted to feel like a man again—strong, capable, whole.

But what he said hit me like a brick wall: "Strength isn't found in pretending you're unbroken. It's found in the courage to rebuild what's been shattered."

That cut deep.

He taught me that healing isn't about rushing past the pain—it's about sitting with it, learning from it, and slowly, brick by brick, mending the cracks. I learned how to ground myself when anxiety clawed at my chest, how to speak truth over lies I'd carried for years, and most importantly, how to forgive—my ex-wife, my father, and myself.

Restoring what was broken wasn't a straight line. I stumbled. I doubted. But every time, I was reminded that healing isn't about perfection but progress.

Now, I'm sober. I'm present in my kids' lives. And for the first time, I feel whole—not because life is perfect, but because I am.

CHAPTER 1

BUILDING A SAFE DAILY ROUTINE

Picture the hush of early morning, the world still caught between sleep and the stirring of a new day. You open your eyes and feel a slight twinge of unease—maybe old memories crowd your mind, or a subtle weight presses on your heart. Before your feet hit the floor, you already sense the usual anxiety creeping in. But now, imagine there's another way. Instead of letting stress hijack your day, you create a gentle practice that grounds you in hope, reminding you of God's steady presence from the start.

One of the most powerful ways to mend the frayed edges of a wounded soul is by weaving small moments of calm into your daily routine. These simple habits become anchors—holding you firm when life's demands try to carry you off-balance. Healing doesn't always arrive in giant leaps;

it often comes in the faithful rhythm of everyday life, where you allow grace to shape the details of your morning, midday, and evening.

Morning can be a tender time, especially if you often wake up with your mind racing and your heart already preparing for conflict or worry. Consider taking a quiet pause instead of racing to check your phone or plunging into a to-do list. Sit at the edge of your bed, close your eyes, and breathe deeply. Whisper a prayer: "Lord, be my center today." Let that prayer align your heart with something greater than your stress. Some mornings, you might open a window and let in the fresh air or flip through a short passage of Scripture that reminds you of God's closeness. This is not about perfection; it's about allowing a few minutes of stillness to soak into your spirit, telling your body and soul, *"We're not rushing into chaos; we're stepping into grace."*

As the day unfolds, you'll find moments—maybe at work, running errands, or caring for family—when tension creeps up unannounced. Instead of bulldozing through, set a gentle midpoint break for yourself. Perhaps you place a reminder on your phone or a note in your planner: *"Midday check-in: how am I feeling?"* Stop for a moment, breathe slowly, and do a quick scan of your body. Are your shoulders bunched up around your neck? Is your jaw clenched? Are your thoughts spiraling? By simply naming what you notice, you disrupt the cycle of tension that often runs on autopilot. Offer a short prayer, like, *"God, ground me now. Let me remember I'm safe."* Even if it's just ninety seconds of intentional calm, that pause can reset your mind, reminding you that no problem is bigger than the One who holds you.

Then comes the winding down at day's end, a period that can be surprisingly challenging if you carry unresolved worry or emotional burdens. You climb into bed, but your mind replays the day's triggers or rehearses tomorrow's potential crises. This is when an evening wind-down practice can protect your rest. Maybe it starts an hour before bedtime: dim the lights, turn off the TV or phone, and replace those screens with something that nurtures peace, like sipping herbal tea, reading something uplifting, or listening to gentle music. Even if you can't fully silence your racing thoughts, you can direct them toward gratitude. Offer thanks for one moment in the day—no matter how small—where you felt hope break through. Light a scented candle, if you like, and whisper, *"Lord, thank You for carrying me another day."* Such an easy practice can remind you that you're cared for and that it's safe to let your guard down and sleep.

These routines aren't superficial bandaids; they're expressions of how you choose to live now that you're mending. Every gentle morning prayer is a statement that yesterday's trauma doesn't own today. Every midday pause declares you won't be driven by the same adrenaline that once fueled your fears. Every quiet evening routine is a stand against the old anxiety that used to stalk your nights. By claiming these small pockets of calm, you nurture your healing from within, telling your nervous system and spirit, *"I am allowed to feel safe. I am choosing to rest in God's care."*

Of course, life doesn't always cooperate with perfect plans. There will be days you oversleep, a crisis arises at noon that interrupts your midday check-in, or a barrage of phone calls disrupts your evening wind-down.

Grace yourself with flexibility. The idea is not to be rigid but to trust that even ten minutes of stillness or five minutes of prayer can shift your internal climate. Over time, these small daily choices accumulate into a robust foundation. You find that your spirit holds more resilience, your faith feels more integrated into your schedule, and your heart experiences less panic and more steadiness.

The Holy Spirit can gently minister to your bruised places in these routines. He's present in that morning breath of air, the midday prayer that regrounds you, the evening reflection that sets your mind on good things. Trauma taught you to live in a perpetual state of alert, but healing teaches you to dwell in a consistent awareness of divine peace. It's not an instant flip of a switch—rather, it's a cultivated habit of letting peace seep into the cracks of your day.

So, as you begin *Mended*, start here. Start by giving yourself permission to carve out these daily habits—moments in the morning, midday, and night that serve as sacred ground. This is where healing moves beyond theory and becomes a lived reality. With each morning practice, you awaken to fresh mercy; with each midday pause, you remind yourself of God's constant presence; with each nighttime routine, you cradle your heart with rest. And slowly, day by day, you'll discover a deeper calm that trauma tried to steal but failed. Let your daily routine tell the story of hope returning, faith standing firm, and a spirit rising stronger than before.

Reflection Questions

1. What small changes can you make in your daily routine to create a sense of safety and stability?

2. How do your current morning or evening routines impact your emotional well-being?

3. What specific practices can help you start and end your day with calm and intention?

4. How do you respond to disruptions in your daily routine, and how can you approach them with more grace?

5. What spiritual or grounding practices can you incorporate to foster peace throughout your day?

CHAPTER 2

GROUNDING TECHNIQUES FOR SUDDEN FEAR

S andra was in the grocery store reaching for a can on a shelf when suddenly she felt a jolt of anxiety seize your body. "My heart began racing, my palms grew damp, and it felt like the world was closing in on me," she explained. She couldn't quite name it, but a deep-rooted alarm blared in her mind: *"Danger—get out!"* This is the surge of sudden fear, the kind that trauma sets on a hair-trigger. Before you realize it, you're ready to abandon your cart and sprint for the exit.

But what if, instead of being swept away by that wave of panic, Sandra had a lifeline—an immediate way to bring herself back to the present, to steady her heart, and to remind her body that she was safe? That's the gift of grounding. It's a series of simple yet powerful tools designed to anchor you in the *now* rather than letting old anxieties hijack your soul.

When trauma lingers in the background, your nervous system stays on high alert, ever ready to flee, fight, or freeze at the faintest sign of threat. This hypervigilance might have saved you once, but now it feels more like a prison. Grounding techniques act like a key, gently freeing you from those invisible chains. They're not about denying your pain or pretending the danger never happened; they're about reminding your mind and body that *today*, in this moment, you are here, and you are secure.

Sometimes, fear strikes so quickly that you can barely form words to pray. Your chest tightens, and you might even forget to breathe. One of the fastest ways to counter this spiral is by focusing on your breath. Find a slow, intentional rhythm. Inhale for a count of four—feeling your lungs fill and your belly expand—then exhale just as slowly, releasing any tension you can sense in your muscles. If you can, whisper something simple to yourself: *"God is with me. I am safe now."* Each measured breath defies the rising panic, guiding your heart back into balance.

Don't underestimate how transformative this simple act can be. A few well-placed breaths can interrupt the thunderstorm of anxiety raging in your mind, letting calm seep into your bloodstream. It might feel unnatural at first—you're used to gulping shallow gasps or holding your breath during distress—but practice will show you how powerfully your body responds to a deliberate, peaceful inhale and exhale.

When sudden fear slams into you, your mind might start spiraling with worst-case scenarios. That's trauma's way of trying to protect you—by anticipating threats that might not even exist. Grounding yourself in the present environment breaks that loop. Take a second to look around. Count the colors you see or name three objects in your immediate vicinity: the rows of cereal boxes, a child's laughter down the aisle, a soft hum of overhead lights. You anchor your thoughts by describing what's real and tangible.

You can also lean on your senses in a more structured way. Touch something textured—like the fabric of your shirt or the cart handle—and notice how it feels beneath your fingertips. Listen for the quietest sound you can hear, whether it's your breath or the distant hum of a cash register. These subtle cues connect you to reality, outsmarting the panic that wants to pull you into the past or a dreaded future. As you consciously engage sight, touch, and hearing, gently tell your body, *"This is where I am. The threat isn't here. I can breathe."*

Have you ever seen a child clutch a blanket or stuffed animal when frightened? Adults often need the same concept, just in a different form. A small cross in your pocket, a note card with a Scripture, or a smooth stone you've prayed over can become a tangible anchor. When fear flares up, you reach for that object, hold it, and recall that you're not alone—that God is near, even in the most chaotic moments.

It might sound too simple—like a child's security blanket—but there's profound reassurance in touching something that represents peace or divine love. It's a physical reminder that you carry comfort wherever you go. You can even whisper a short prayer or affirmation each time you touch it: *"Lord, still my heart. I trust Your protection."* Repetition helps cement that calm into your instincts, making it easier to lean on this practice the next time panic attempts to steal your breath.

God is not absent when your heart pounds out of control. In fact, Scripture reminds us that He is an ever-present help in times of trouble. Grounding techniques are a tool, but faith is the backbone. When you pair a soothing breath with a silent prayer— *"Jesus, be near to me"*—you bring the presence of the Almighty into your exact moment of crisis. Suddenly, that grocery store aisle or crowded bus stop is transformed from a battlefield into holy ground, where fear and faith collide, and faith can prevail.

This doesn't mean you won't feel anxious. It means you have a path out of anxiety's grip. Fear may still knock at the door, but you learn you're not obligated to invite it in for tea. Sometimes, a single whispered verse—like, *"God is my refuge and strength, a very present help in trouble"*—can open the door to peace. Over time, it can become second nature: fear arises, you acknowledge it, and you respond with breath, sensory grounding, or a comforting object in hand, along with a prayer that reaffirms your spirit.

As I said, these techniques might feel awkward the first few times you apply them—especially if panic used to take you by storm without a second thought. But just like any skill, grounding gets easier and more effective with repetition. You'll find your confidence quietly blooming the next time anxious thoughts start creeping in. It's like having a shield ready. Fear might still break over you, but it no longer has the same power to pull you under. You catch it early, breathe, focus your senses, cling to your comfort object, and recenter yourself in God's steadfast love.

Consider practicing grounding even when you're not anxious—maybe for a minute or two each morning. You'll be teaching your body and brain this new language of calm so that when the storm hits, you're already fluent in its vocabulary. Over time, you'll feel a shift: your body becomes less prone to lurching into panic, and your spirit stays more rooted in faith than in old trauma triggers.

These grounding techniques aren't magic potions that erase all fear forever. Trauma may linger, and triggers may still ambush you once in a while. But each time you practice, each time you choose to root yourself in the moment instead of letting anxiety spiral, you're chipping away at the hold trauma once had on your life. It's the daily act of reasserting control over your body, mind, and spirit, all under God's grace.

Let's return to that moment in the grocery store again: Sarah's heart pounds, her knees threaten to buckle, but she recalls that she has the tools *and* a loving Father who stands with her. She slows your breath, names three objects around her, grasps her comforting cross in her hand-bag pocket, and whispers, *"I am safe. God is here. Fear will not drown me."* Slowly, the tide of panic recedes. She wipes the sweat from her brow, and with a steady heart, she moves forward. Isn't this outcome a better option than running out of the grocery store in panic? You can have a better outcome also. I sincerely hope and pray that in your everyday, unassuming moment, you will choose to heal over helplessness—and that, my friend, is victory at its finest.

Reflection Questions

1. When fear suddenly overwhelms you, what grounding techniques help you return to the present moment?

2. How does your body physically react to fear, and what calming methods can you use to soothe it?

3. What role does your faith play in helping you navigate moments of sudden anxiety?

4. Have you identified specific triggers that heighten your fear? How can you respond differently when they occur?

5. What grounding practices can you use in public or high-stress environments to maintain calm?

CHAPTER 3

REPLACING HARMFUL THOUGHTS

H ave you ever been in a quiet room when a negative thought barged in, uninvited, and turned your peace upside down? You sit there, minding your own business, and suddenly, a whisper says, *"You're a failure,"* or *"Nothing will ever change for you."* It's like a thief slipping in through a window you forgot to lock, stealing the confidence you worked so hard to build. These harmful thoughts often stem from old patterns, remnants of trauma, or a lifetime of criticism that lodged themselves in your mind. But here's the truth: if those thoughts can be planted, they can also be uprooted.

Overcoming harmful self-talk is like tending a garden after a harsh storm. Weeds of lies may have taken root, but with consistent pruning and replanting, you can develop a flourishing space filled with grace and truth. It doesn't happen overnight and requires more than just a passing wish for something better. But with the right tools and God's guiding presence, you can gradually transform the very landscape of your mind, pulling out the weeds of lies and deception and planting seeds of life-giving truth.

First, you must learn to spot these harmful thoughts. They often disguise themselves as your internal voice, saying things like, "I always mess everything up," or "I'm never going to be okay." Maybe you've grown so accustomed to these statements that you think they're facts. But a lie repeated doesn't magically become truth. Trauma can magnify every small mistake and every bit of rejection until you believe your entire identity is worthless. But, friend, that's not the voice of the One who formed you. God calls you beloved, chosen, and redeemed. The question is: which voice will you believe?

Begin paying attention to your mental chatter. Notice when a thought causes a heavy drop in your chest or a wave of discouragement in your spirit. If it's loaded with words like "always" and "never," that's often a clue it's an exaggerated lie. Write it down if you can, giving that thought a name. This is the moment you pull it into the light of honesty, refusing to let it hide in the unspoken corners of your mind.

Once you've identified a harmful thought—"I'm incapable of real progress," "No one cares about me," or "I am unlovable"—don't leave it hanging in the air. Confront it with the truth. Think of it as a courtroom scene: the negative voice stands up, accusing you of failure or worthlessness, but you bring forth your evidence: a faith-rooted, reality-based rebuttal that says, "This is not who I am, and here's why."

That rebuttal might be a specific memory of how you managed a trigger or overcame a challenge. It could be a comforting Scripture that declares your worth, such as *"I am fearfully and wonderfully made."* Or it could be a heartfelt note from a friend who believes in you. Whatever truth you use, let it directly oppose the lie. The idea isn't to ignore the negative voice but to replace it with something far more solid and uplifting. Over time, you train your brain to reach for facts and faith rather than spiraling into doubt.

There's tremendous power in vocalizing truth. When a harmful thought tells you, *"I'm doomed to fail,"* try saying aloud, "No, I am learning and growing every day, and I can do all things through Christ who strengthens me." Hearing your own voice declare a better reality solidifies that statement. It's like planting a signpost in your mind that reads, *"Trauma's lies stop here."*

You might initially feel awkward—like you're just talking to yourself. But in the spiritual realm, your spoken words hold weight. Isn't it written that life and death lie in the power of the tongue? You activate that promise by voicing affirmations that align with God's Word. You're no longer passively accepting every harsh whisper that drifts through your thoughts; instead, you're stepping into the gatekeeper role, discerning which messages get to enter and which must be turned away.

When replacing lies, Scripture can be a wellspring of truth. It's like a reservoir of living water you can draw from at any moment. If your inner critic keeps shouting, "You're too broken to ever be loved," combat it with verses like *"The Lord is close to the brokenhearted"* or *"Nothing can separate us from the love of God."* Suddenly, you're not just arguing with a negative voice in your strength but invoking divine authority. This can move mountains of doubt faster than you'd imagine.

Find a handful of verses that speak directly to your areas of struggle, whether it's shame, fear, or a deep sense of inadequacy. Write them on sticky notes, put them on your bathroom mirror, or store them on your phone. Please make a point of reciting them, especially during times when old beliefs rear their heads. With repetition, you'll find the truth becomes ingrained, and you'll reach for Scripture reflexively whenever negativity flares.

Think of your mind as a stage: for years, self-critical thoughts might have played the lead role, with doubt and fear as the supporting cast. But now you're rewriting the script. You need to repeatedly rehearse your new lines to shift that internal narrative. Don't expect a single declaration of truth to undo decades of negative thinking. Consciously speak or journal a healthier narrative about who you are becoming each day.

Try something simple: each morning, say or write down three statements of truth about yourself. For example, "I am learning to rest in God's grace. I have survived so much and am stronger than I used to be. My past does not dictate my future." Again, it might feel forced initially, but as you commit to it, these new lines become second nature. Over time, negativity finds less and less room to occupy your mental stage because it's already filled with affirmations rooted in truth and faith.

Please pay attention to casual phrases you toss around, like "I'm such an idiot" or "I never do anything right." Those small statements feed harmful thoughts by reinforcing a distorted self-image. Instead, practice kinder self-talk, even in the simple mistakes. Instead of "I messed up again," say, "I'm human, and I can learn from this." Instead of "I'll never change," try, "I might need more time, but I'm moving forward." These shifts might seem minor, but they compound into a broader, healthier narrative that shapes how you see yourself and your potential.

Also, be mindful of the language you allow from others. If someone consistently speaks down to you or mocks your struggles, consider whether you need more precise boundaries or a different environment. No matter how strong your internal work is, a toxic daily environment can undermine it. You are expected to guard your heart, especially when you're in a season of reclaiming truth over your mind.

So, why is all this effort necessary? Because destructive thoughts can hold you back from healing more effectively than any external obstacle. You might do all the proper steps—counseling, journaling, setting boundaries—but if your mind is constantly berating you, you'll struggle to believe authentic wholeness is possible. On the other hand, when you begin to take control of your thoughts, you find momentum in every other area of recovery. Suddenly, triggers feel less powerful, boundaries feel more natural, and faith feels less abstract.

Replacing harmful thoughts is like changing the filter through which you see yourself and the world. Where you once saw only darkness and defeat, you start noticing glimmers of possibility. Where you thought

God was distant, you sense His closeness in your daily walk. Where you believed you were beyond help, you now see someone worthy of compassion and growth.

Changing your thought patterns is a labor of love—love for yourself, the life God intended for you, and ultimately, love for the One who calls you to heal. Every time you correct a lie with truth, you're placing another brick on the path out of trauma's shadow. Remember, you don't walk this journey alone. The Holy Spirit stands ready to remind you of life's words, empower you when you feel weary, and celebrate each mental breakthrough you achieve.

So keep nurturing those new beliefs. Keep letting go of the old lies that say you're stuck, hopeless, or unlovable. Each small victory in your mind paves the way for lasting transformation. In God's eyes, you have always been loved, created with purpose, and destined for freedom. Now is your chance to align your thoughts with that unshakeable truth. Over time, you'll see that what once bound your mind in chains is replaced by confidence forged in faith and a new song declaring: *"I am redeemed, I am whole, and my thoughts will no longer be my enemies."*

Reflection Questions

1. What recurring negative thoughts do you struggle with, and where might they have originated?

2. How can you replace harmful self-talk with affirmations rooted in truth and faith?

3. What role does Scripture play in reshaping your internal dialogue?

4. How do your thoughts influence your emotions and actions, and what shifts could bring healing?

5. What practical steps can you take to interrupt negative thinking patterns when they arise?

CHAPTER 4

SMALL STEPS TOWARD TRUSTING OTHERS

C lose your eyes briefly and remember when you felt the sting of broken trust. It might have been a careless word from a friend, a promise someone made but never kept, or a betrayal that left you wondering if you could ever open your heart again. Trauma intensifies these experiences—every ounce of hurt from the past can settle over your present like a dark cloud, whispering, "Don't get too close, or you'll be hurt again." Yet deep in your soul, you long for connection. You want to believe there is goodness in people and that healthy relationships can bring healing instead of more pain.

Relearning how to trust is not an overnight affair. It's an intricate, step-by-step journey of letting down your guard in measured ways, testing the ground to see if it can support your heart again. Think of a child standing by a pool's edge—tentatively dipping a toe, then a foot, gauging the water's temperature before going deeper. Trust works the same way. After you've been bruised or wounded, you don't just leap into the deep end. You approach connection with caution, building it layer by layer.

Maybe you've put up walls so high you don't even notice them anymore—they've become the background of how you live. You keep conversations shallow or avoid situations that require vulnerability. It feels safer to manage life on your own than risk another heartbreak. But what if that isolation costs you a deeper level of comfort, support, and genuine love? God designed us for relationships, to bear each other's burdens, and to experience the joy of companionship. The challenge is learning to open ourselves to that design without letting past wounds define every new interaction.

If you're holding onto the belief that all people are untrustworthy, begin by identifying one person in your life who has shown kindness or reliability. Maybe it's a longtime friend who's never judged your anxieties or a mentor who's patiently listened. Start by sharing a small piece of your story or a mild concern—something that matters but not the deepest secret you hold. Observe how they respond to you. Do they listen without jumping to conclusions? Do they maintain confidentiality, or do they pass it along as gossip? This first step isn't about sneakily testing them; it's about gathering evidence that not everyone will treat your heart casually. Often, you'll find that a trustworthy response—one given with compassion and respect—can loosen the grip of fear on your soul.

Trauma often plants a chorus of "what if" voices in your mind: "What if they use this against me? What if they don't understand? What if they leave me once they see my scars?" These voices keep you locked in self-protection mode. But faith calls you to challenge them. Scripture reveals a God who never leaves or forsakes you. While we are imperfect, we are still capable of reflecting divine love. By taking small relational risks, you allow yourself to experience kindness from another, thereby rewriting the old script that says you must always handle burdens alone.

Trusting others doesn't mean swinging from total withdrawal to total exposure overnight. Healthy trust thrives together with healthy boundaries. You can share a slice of vulnerability without giving away the entire cake. Boundaries are not walls that keep everyone out; they're gates that let the right people in. They define where your comfort zone lies, ensuring that when you reach beyond it, you do so deliberately and under the guidance of wisdom and faith.

For instance, if you confide in someone, it's okay to say, "I'd like to share something personal, but please keep it between us for now." If they honor that boundary, it's a sign of respect for your trust. If they dismiss or violate it, then you know where you stand. Though painful, that clarity prevents deeper harm down the road. Over time, you'll learn which ones consistently honor your boundaries and which ones you must keep at arm's length. This discernment might feel like a skill you never fully developed, especially if past relationships eroded your ability to recognize red flags. But with every mindful interaction, you sharpen that skill, growing more confident in who you let into your healing process.

Faith-based communities—like a small group at church or an online fellowship—can also provide a structured environment for rebuilding trust. Often, these groups gather under the premise of mutual support and spiritual growth, offering a safer space to share. By hearing other people's testimonies of how they overcame trauma or heartbreak, you start to see that your struggles are not unique and your fears are not insurmountable. Those glimpses of shared humanity can be profoundly comforting: *"They've been hurt too, yet they're still here, finding hope and strength."* In time, you might open up about your journey, discovering that the same grace that carried them can carry you.

One of the most reassuring truths about trusting others is that God remains your unshakable foundation. Even if you risk opening up and someone mishandles that vulnerability, the Lord's presence does not waver. He sees every tear, every attempt you make to connect, every disappointment, and every victory. Think of Him as a loving Father, standing behind you as you carefully take steps toward building new friendships or mending old ones. If a stumble happens, He catches you, reminding you that earthly rejections do not define your ultimate worth.

As you nurture trust, draw courage from prayer. Before opening up about a sensitive issue, pause and say, "God, give me wisdom. Guide my words, guide their response, and help me trust Your protection." This prayer frames your vulnerability not as an act of helplessness but as a faith-fueled decision to embrace community despite the risk. Over time, you'll realize that while we may falter, God's hand holds you steady, ensuring that no betrayal can truly break you.

Now, the first time you share a piece of your story—even if it's just a tiny snippet—acknowledge the bravery it takes. If the person responds with empathy, celebrate the connection that brings. If they react poorly, celebrate the clarity you gained about that relationship. Both outcomes teach you something valuable. Trusting others isn't about guaranteeing every encounter will be perfect; it's about refusing to let fear decide your fate.

The more you practice this intentional, bounded vulnerability, the easier it becomes. Slowly, new friendships might form. Old relationships, once fragile, might find a second wind as understanding and compassion grow. Painful relationships may still have to be released, but even that releasing can be a healing step—acknowledging that not everyone is meant to journey with you into your new season.

Eventually, trusting others again is not about glossing over your scars or pretending the betrayal never happened. It's about deciding your life will not be ruled by fear or suspicion. It's about daring to believe in something bigger than your wounds. Think of the disciples in Scripture: they faced persecution, betrayal, and loss, yet they kept forming communities and leaning on one another and the God who called them. Faith empowered them to see each other's flaws and still build unity. That same faith can empower you to see beyond the failures of your past and envision a future where genuine relationships uplift and enrich your life.

As you integrate these steps—choosing the right person to confide in, setting healthy boundaries, leaning on faith for courage—take note of your progress. Maybe a month from now, you'll realize you've begun sharing more freely, or your anxiety about closeness has decreased. That's the beauty of growth: it sneaks up on you in the most ordinary moments. Where you once felt alone and locked behind protective walls, you now find rays of light streaming in, warming your spirit with the realization that you can let love in again.

So, go forward with courage. Let each small step toward trusting others be a testament that trauma may have tried to isolate you, but love, community, and faith are stronger forces. You stand on God's promise that He'll never leave you, so you are never unshielded, even in the vulnerability of extending your heart. And as you see the fruits of new connections, let gratitude fill your heart—gratitude that healing can indeed bloom in the soil where hurt once took root. Keep walking. You're closer to wholeness than you've ever been.

Reflection Questions

1. How has past trauma affected your ability to trust others?

2. What small, intentional steps can you take to rebuild trust in safe relationships?

3. What boundaries can you establish to create healthier connections?

4. How can you discern between people who foster growth and those who drain your energy?

5. What role does community play in your healing process, and how can you lean into it more fully?

CHAPTER 5

EMBRACING QUIET MOMENTS

In our fast-paced world, silence is becoming a rare and precious gift. We rush from one obligation to the next, filling every spare second with noise—our phones, tasks, and worries. We have become accustomed to the noise, and we are oblivious to the fact that there's a gentle secret hidden in the stillness that often goes unnoticed, especially when you're carrying the echoes of trauma in your soul. That secret is simply this: sometimes, the quiet can heal what endless activities cannot. Sadly, many of us don't know how to embrace this life-enhancing quiet. Embracing quiet moments is about stepping away from the chatter and allowing a deeper form of rest to cradle your mind, heart, and body.

It may seem paradoxical. Trauma survivors sometimes avoid silence because it's in the hush that old memories resurface, that anxious thoughts grow louder. In the stillness, there's nowhere to run. But this act of being still, if approached with grace, can become a sanctified space where you learn to be present without letting past wounds dictate your entire state of being. Think of it as slowly entering a peaceful garden. The first time you walk in, you might notice weeds—unwanted thoughts that tried to take root while you were busy. But, suppose you keep returning to that garden, tending it gently. In that case, you discover blossoms of clarity and peace that surprise you.

Most of us don't stumble upon silence; we must choose it. This might mean waking up ten minutes earlier to sit quietly with a mug of tea or slipping outside to watch the sunset without scrolling through our phones. These moments of chosen stillness allow your nervous system to exhale, to release tension it clung to all day. Picture yourself stepping onto a quiet porch: there's no pressure to say or solve anything. You breathe, noticing the rustle of leaves or the gentle hum of distant traffic. In that simple act, you give your soul permission to calm down. You shift from chaos to calm.

Faith can thrive in such spaces. You're more likely to sense God's presence without the noise of constantly doing. A short prayer in the stillness—"Lord, I'm here, and I trust You"—can anchor you more than a hundred rushed words said in passing. Silence is the soil where intimate communion with God often sprouts. You may feel your heart rate steady, your shoulders descend from around your ears, and a subtle awareness of God's reassurance takes root.

For many trauma survivors, silence isn't synonymous with peace at first. It can be unsettling—like turning down the background music in a room to suddenly hear your heartbeat. Thoughts and worries you pushed aside now wander to the forefront. Old wounds might knock on your consciousness, demanding to be felt or acknowledged. That discomfort can tempt you to abandon quiet moments altogether. But here's the grace: gently staying put in that hush teaches your mind and body that those old feelings need not overwhelm you. You can breathe through them and allow them to exist without dictating your every move.

It helps to have a simple grounding practice when the silence stirs anxiety. For instance, you might place a hand over your heart, slowly inhaling and exhaling, repeating a short phrase like, "I'm safe, I'm here, God is here." This anchors you in the moment, reminding you that although past pains exist, they are not the entire story. As time passes, you'll find that the quiet ceases to be a battlefield and becomes a place of refuge. On this spot, you can reconcile your fears with the comfort of divine compassion.

We often neglect what's happening internally because we're too busy externally. Embracing quiet moments can become a discipline of self-awareness. Maybe once a day, you pause for five minutes—turn off notifications, close the door, and sit. Ask yourself, "How am I doing really?" Notice if tension hides in your shoulders or sadness lingers beneath a forced smile. Sometimes, trauma pushes you to ignore these subtle signals. But in silence, they gently come to the surface. You may realize you're more anxious about tomorrow's meeting than you admitted or still upset about an earlier conversation.

Naming these feelings—*I'm anxious, sad, frustrated*—isn't about wallowing; it's about letting your inner truth breathe. Once named, you can pray over them, journal them out, or share them with someone supportive. Silence thus becomes a mirror reflecting your emotional landscape so you can address it with intention and faith rather than letting unresolved emotions pile up like clutter in a back room.

Consider establishing small routines that frame your day with silence. It could be as simple as lighting a candle before bedtime, sitting in stillness for a few minutes, and letting the soft glow remind you of God's enduring light. Or take a short walk outdoors—no headphones, just the symphony of nature or the hum of the city around you. Let each step become a communion with the present moment. Suppose you're inclined to prayer or meditation. In that case, this is an ideal time to whisper your heart's concerns or rest in the awareness of God's presence without a list of demands.

In these practices, trauma's frantic voices lose some of their volume. They don't vanish entirely, but they no longer get to dominate the conversation. You create a space where you reclaim ownership of your thoughts, breath, and body. You affirm, "I am not just a sum of what happened; I am a person who can connect deeply with the gift of stillness."

Throughout Scripture, we see moments where even Jesus withdrew to solitude—a wilderness, a mountainside—to pray and be alone. If the Son of God took time to step away from crowds and noise, how much more might you, in your healing journey, benefit from these pockets of silence? We often preach about worship music or dynamic sermons. But there is a quieter side to spirituality: letting God speak to you in the hush. When you quiet the external racket, you position your heart to hear the gentle whisper of divine love and truth, guiding you toward your next step in healing.

This spiritual reset can also be a balm when triggers have worn you down. After a wave of anxiety, you might carve out ten minutes to be silent in God's presence, letting Him restore your soul. It's like stepping into a refreshing stream on a scorching day. You don't have to be eloquent or muster elaborate prayers; your presence is enough. In that moment, you surrender your weariness, allowing the Spirit to mend frayed nerves and soothe raw emotions.

You might be wondering, *"What difference will silence make? Isn't therapy or medication or action more important?"* Those can all be vital, yes. But silence is the fertile soil in which the seeds of your healing take root. Over time, you'll notice the fruit it bears. Perhaps you become less reactive in situations that used to set you on edge. Maybe you find new clarity about personal issues you've been wrestling with. You might even discover a deeper sense of God's closeness. This assurance extends beyond intellectual belief into a felt reality.

Embracing quiet moments doesn't mean you stop wrestling with your thoughts. But it does mean you create an arena where those thoughts can surface, be acknowledged, and gently guided by faith and self-compassion. It's the difference between your mind being a noisy marketplace and becoming a serene chapel. The same issues may appear, but in the calm of that chapel, you can address them with more wisdom and grace.

Lastly, recognize that this journey might take courage. If silence feels threatening because of traumatic memories, start small. A minute or two at first, gradually building up. Use supportive practices—like a simple grounding or reading a comforting verse—before and after your silent time. Invite a trusted friend or counselor to walk alongside you if the quiet unearths deeper pains. Over time, you may find the very place you once dreaded—silence—becomes a sanctuary of healing.

In that sanctuary, your heart learns a fresh rhythm, no longer beating solely to the drum of fear or the roar of old echoes. In that sanctuary, you discover how to live calmer, how to treat your own emotions with compassion, and how to hear the still, small voice of God reminding you, day after day, "You are not defined by your scars. You are safe here. You are loved."

So begin with a simple moment of silence today. Let it be an invitation rather than a threat, a gentle pause that ushers in peace. No matter how broken or busy you've felt, allow the quiet to cradle you in God's arms. Let this be one more stepping stone on the path from *scarred* to *mended*, reminding you that genuine restoration can *bloom* in stillness.

Reflection Questions

1. How do you currently view moments of silence? Are they restful or unsettling?

2. In what ways can quiet moments become spaces for reflection and healing?

3. What practices help you embrace solitude without feeling isolated?

4. How can you turn down external noise to better hear your inner voice and God's guidance?

5. What fears or emotions surface in silence, and how can you process them with grace?

CHAPTER 6

GENTLE MOVEMENT AND YOUR BODY

Take a mental journey with me. Imagine a serene morning when the sun filters through your window. For the first time in a while, you notice your body asking for gentle care instead of bracing for the day's demands. For those who carry wounds, the body can feel like a battlefield—tense muscles, stiff shoulders, racing heart. But what if this body, which you once saw as a vessel of tension or distress, could become an instrument of calm and prayer? That's the gift of gentle movement. Gentle movement can be a new lens through which you let your body breathe and heal, guided by a steady, healing hand.

We often forget how deeply our bodies absorb our hurts. Trauma doesn't just create emotional turmoil; it can also lodge in our physical frame, leaving us with chronic tightness in the neck or an unexplainable ache in the lower back. Some days, you might feel like every muscle is on high alert, a silent echo of past battles. Yet, God crafted us with remarkable resilience. The same body that clenches at the memory of pain can also be taught a new movement of release and rest. Gentle movement is a way to honor that resilience—allowing tension to loosen and ushering in a calmness that anxiety tried to steal.

Now, gentle movement doesn't require an elaborate gym routine or hours of intense workouts. It starts with something as simple as stretching. Picture yourself waking up and rolling your shoulders gently backward, noticing how the knots unravel just a little. Maybe you lift your arms overhead and feel a slow, satisfying release across your back. This isn't about perfect form; it's about whispering to your body: *"It's okay. We don't have to be on guard right now."* At that moment, each stretch is more than a physical act; it becomes a statement of faith that you don't have to live perpetually tightened against invisible threats. You're allowed to greet the day with openness.

Walking outdoors can magnify that sense of release. Let your steps be unhurried, almost contemplative, as if you're taking a prayer walk without saying a word. Notice the gentle sway of your arms, how your feet connect with the ground and the rhythm of your breathing. The world might be rushing by—cars zooming, people chatting—but you're cultivating a space of peace in motion. Some days, you might only manage a short walk down the street. On other days, you may roam a local park. The length doesn't matter nearly as much as the intention. The intention is to let your body move in harmony rather than tension, to let nature remind you that renewal is woven into creation. Leaves change, seasons shift, and so can we.

Even in this movement, faith can come alive. Instead of letting your mind race with to-do lists or replays of old hurts, focus on each breath as a small prayer: *"Lord, let me feel Your peace in this step... Lord, quiet the storms in my soul."* Eventually, this discipline of walking slowly and deliberately transforms from a casual stroll into an act of worship. You might find that what used to be a swirl of anxious thoughts calms down as you immerse yourself in the present moment. The breeze against your skin, the steady pulse of your heartbeat, the subtle sense of God's hand guiding each footfall; these are evidence that you are mending.

Then there's a beautiful concept I like to call "movement as prayer in action." Have you ever considered that every gentle sway, every stretch, every measured step can be a conversation with God? You might raise your arms out wide as if to say, "Here I am, Lord—receiving Your grace." You might bow slightly in a posture of surrender, acknowledging that your wounds and worries are not too heavy for His hands. In those brief, mindful acts, your body becomes a living, moving prayer. It's not about performance; it's about inviting the Holy Spirit into the language of your muscles and bones.

For those who've lived with trauma, hearing "listen to your body" might sound foreign. It might even sound counterproductive. After all, your body was the bearer of so many unwanted memories. But gentle movement invites a new dialogue. Instead of expecting your body to flinch at every noise or brace for the next blow, you guide it toward restfulness.

You teach it that not every movement has to be about defending danger. Slowly letting your body learn the truth that it's possible to be safe, to dwell in a space of calm rather than constant vigilance, you reclaim the lifestyle that trauma stole from you.

If you're worried about doing it "right," banish that thought. This isn't a competition. It could be five minutes of stretching after brushing your teeth, a ten-minute walk at lunchtime, or some gentle arm and neck rolls before bed while whispering a short prayer. The point isn't to impress anyone; it's to create a daily practice that reminds your system: *"I can release tension. I can let go of fear."*

You'll notice subtle but profound changes as you develop these gentle movements. Those knots in your shoulders might not stay as tight. Once clenched through every stressful moment, your jaw may gradually find its ease. You start to breathe deeper, no longer holding your breath in anticipation of the worst. And there, in the quiet shift of your physical posture, you also find a window opening into emotional and spiritual rest.

Some days, you might not feel like moving at all. That's okay. The process of trauma recovery has its ups and downs, and sometimes, just lying still with slow, deliberate breathing is enough. Remember, the goal isn't to force your body but to gently invite it out of its defensive crouch. Even a tiny step is a victory. Each day, you're rewriting old narratives that said your body was forever locked in tension. You're telling your muscles and mind that you're walking toward healing, step by tender step.

Don't forget to anchor all this in prayer or a short reflection. Before you stretch, you might say, *"God, guide this movement. Help me release what I no longer need to carry."* As you walk, think, *"Each step is a move away from my past hurts and toward the peace You promise."* If you choose to raise your arms in a posture of praise, let it be an outward sign of an inward longing for wholeness. If you bow your head in gratitude, let it acknowledge that your strength is nurtured by the God who loves us unconditionally.

Gentle movement invites you to treat your body as a friend rather than an adversary. Trauma convinced you to see your body as a site of pain or betrayal, but by moving thoughtfully and kindly, you restore it to the role it was meant to play: a temple, a vessel of God's breath, a living testament to resilience. With each movement, you declare that the old chain of extreme alertness is weakening, and a new chain of compassion and faith is taking place.

So begin with what's feasible. Stretch in your living room. Take a short walk in your neighborhood. If you feel inspired, incorporate some music or a whispered psalm. The key is consistency, faith, and gentleness. Over time, you'll sense the synergy between body and spirit, glowing brighter, less overshadowed by old trauma, and more illuminated by renewed hope. And as you lean into that gentle sway of possibility, your body, once battered by tension, can rediscover the pulse of rest.

Reflection Questions

1. How does your body hold stress and trauma, and what gentle movements help release tension?

2. What physical activities bring you a sense of peace and grounding?

3. How can you integrate mindful movement into your daily routine?

4. What messages has your body been sending you, and how can you respond with compassion?

5. How does movement help reconnect your body and spirit in your healing journey?

CHAPTER 7

REDISCOVERING JOY IN SIMPLE THINGS

Think back to your younger days—perhaps there was a time when you'd catch fireflies on a summer evening or break into laughter over a silly joke without a care in the world. Traumatic experiences often snuff out that sense of wonder, leaving us numb to life's simpler pleasures. To put it bluntly, we no longer get joy and contentment from the things that once brought us joy and happiness. Trauma has made some of us callous of the things that once brought us joy and laughter. But here's the truth: joy was never meant to be a distant memory; it can be rediscovered, gently developed like a forgotten garden now in full bloom. Sometimes, the antidote to life's heaviness is hidden in the smallest delights—a warm cup of tea, a favorite song, or sunlight dancing on your kitchen floor.

Trauma, in its quiet or violent forms, convinces you that each day must be an exercise in survival. But survival is not the same as living. *Living* involves looking up at the sky after weeks of rain and feeling a spark of awe at the clouds parting. It's noticing the scent of fresh bread or the delight in a child's laughter and letting yourself bask in that moment. If you've been weighed down by anxiety, shame, or grief, you may have forgotten how such small joys can lift your spirit. I intend to resurrect that memory—reminding your heart that even if life has been harsh, hope can bloom through tiny cracks of beauty.

When you're accustomed to bracing for the worst, noticing life's tender gifts can be challenging. But the first step to rediscovering joy is training your mind to notice. Maybe you could start by writing down one simple pleasure each day. It could be the moment you sank into your armchair with a novel, the golden hue of morning light, or the feeling of taking off your shoes after a long day. Identifying these small sparks isn't frivolous; it's a practical discipline that reorients you away from trauma's shadows and toward evidence of God's ongoing grace.

You might think, *"But my problems are huge. Focusing on a cup of coffee or a bird chirping outside my window won't fix them."* That's true—small joys don't eliminate big issues. Yet they anchor your spirit in something beyond your pain, reminding you that life can hold both sorrow and sweetness. Each time you acknowledge a tiny blessing, you declare that trauma doesn't command every inch of your emotional territory. God's presence finds a way to show up in these little wonders if only you make space for them.

If you've lost track of what once made your face light up, try dipping your toes back into a hobby that used to spark joy—a childhood pastime, a craft you abandoned, or a creative outlet you always wanted to explore. Maybe you once loved painting, singing, gardening, or journaling your daydreams. Trauma might have robbed the motivation or energy needed to enjoy those pursuits. But it doesn't have to rob them forever.

Start small. If you once enjoyed sketching, buy a cheap notepad and some pencils. Spend ten minutes doodling without judging the outcome. If you love music, play a favorite song and let yourself sway, even if it's just a slow shuffle across the living room. At first, your mind might protest—*"Why bother? This won't solve my bigger issues."* But as you gently reengage with activities that once brought you pleasure, your spirit can breathe again. It's like reopening a window in a stuffy room, letting fresh air displace old stagnation.

Trauma trains you to see what's broken. Joy teaches you to notice what's working, what's beautiful, even if it's small. Another way to rediscover joy is by celebrating your small victories. Did you handle a stressful phone call without losing your cool? Did you clean a corner of your house that's been overwhelming you for months? Please write it down and take a moment to applaud yourself because you did something that chipped away at the stronghold of fear or inactivity.

You might be tempted to dismiss these victories as too small. But honoring them is part of reclaiming your life. Each success—no matter how trivial—reveals a glimmer of your resilience. You might light a candle and say, *"I thank God for giving me the strength to make that tough decision today."* Infusing gratitude into your routine can shift the atmosphere of your mind, warming it with appreciation rather than letting the cold wind of despair blow through all your thoughts.

It's true; some joys are best when shared. If trauma isolates you, consider inviting a friend or loved one to join you in a simple activity—maybe a leisurely walk by a lake, baking cookies in your kitchen, or watching a family-friendly comedy that makes you both laugh until your sides hurt. There's something healing about letting someone else witness your unguarded smile, about seeing their eyes sparkle in response to yours. Where trauma says, *"Stay alone, stay hidden,"* community says, *"Laugh with me. Let's remember life can be good together."*

Church fellowships, small groups, or community hobbies also provide a broader sense of shared joy. Maybe there's a local book club or a faith-based group that meets for casual gatherings. Being around others seeking light in their battles reminds you that your scars don't disqualify you from laughter and connection. In such spaces, the heaviness of your past may seem less stifling, allowing new, joyful memories to unfold.

We often turn to God in our distress, which is good. But what if we also turned to Him in our joy? That's the essence of a relationship: sharing not just our tears but also our laughter. When you notice a moment that makes your heart spark—be it the first sip of morning coffee or a funny text from a friend—pause and acknowledge God's presence. A quick prayer, *"Lord, thank You for this glimpse of light,"* can anchor the experience in gratitude. Over time, these small prayers of thanks create a heart of worship, where you see God's fingerprints in the simpler details of life.

Scripture often points to joy as a fruit of God's Spirit and a declaration of faith. Even in the Old Testament, Nehemiah tells people, "The joy of the Lord is your strength." That's not just a phrase for holiday cards; it's a real force that sustains you in life's valleys. Rediscovering joy is not about denying your trauma or ignoring the scars; it's about letting divine joy dwell alongside your pain, brightening it with possibility, and refusing to let despair dominate every page of your story.

As you reawaken to life's simple pleasures, remember that this isn't a one-time fix. Trauma might still intrude, and triggers may still pull at you. But each moment of joy reminds you that you are more than the sum of your wounds. With time, you might be surprised how these small pockets of delight accumulate into a more hopeful outlook, making the dark clouds pass quicker and the recovery road feel less bleak.

Write down each joyful observation, each tiny triumph. Let these entries become a testament to the resilience God planted in you. Reread them on days when you feel numb when old anxieties return, and see how many bright spots you've collected. This record can rekindle hope, proving that while sorrow has a voice, it doesn't speak for your entire existence.

So, don't overlook that butterfly resting on the flower outside or the sweet crunch of the warm cookie that just came out of the oven. Don't rush past your dog's excited, wagging tail when you come home. Don't dismiss the warmth of a hug or the relief of fresh sheets on your bed.

These everyday wonders can be portals to joy—each one a gentle reminder that pain hasn't erased the goodness woven into creation.

Set your heart free in small increments, welcoming wonder and gratitude. Before you know it, the invisible walls trauma built around your ability to feel will start crumbling. You'll laugh more readily. You'll pause more often to soak in beauty. And you'll realize that in your healing journey, God has been rekindling a joy that can stand alongside your struggles, not denying them but lighting them with a hope that resonates deeper than any darkness you've known.

From morning's first beam of sunlight to the final quiet moments before sleep, invite joy to show up in large and small ways. Turn your heart toward the God who loves to see His children smile, and discover anew that joy is not a luxury for the unscarred; it's an inheritance for every soul brave enough to see grace in life's simplest gifts.

Reflection Questions

1. What simple pleasures bring you unexpected joy, and how can you savor them more often?

2. How can you slow down to notice beauty in the ordinary moments of life?

3. What childhood joys or hobbies can you revisit to reignite your sense of wonder?

4. How does gratitude help shift your focus from survival to thriving?

5. What role does playfulness have in your healing process?

CHAPTER 8

SPEAKING YOUR TRUTH WITH COURAGE

Have you ever felt your voice tighten in your throat right when you wanted to speak? Perhaps you needed to tell someone that their words cut too deep or that you needed help. But right at that moment, trauma whispered loudly, *"Don't cause a fuss,"* or *"No one wants to hear your truth."* This teaches you to stay silent in the face of pain, leaving you with frustration, fear, and resentment. But there's a holy boldness that can set you free when you learn to speak—honestly, directly, without apology. That boldness doesn't mean shouting or being harsh; it means standing in the dignity God gave you and admitting, *"I have needs. I have boundaries. My feelings matter."*

Your voice matters more than you might believe. Suppose you've been conditioned to think your opinions are burdens or that your requests for respect are inconveniences. In that case, you might have grown quiet to maintain peace. But that peace is often a fragile illusion. Inside, your heart aches because your truth stays locked away. Speaking your truth, whether a slight preference or a deep hurt, reaffirms that you exist as more than someone else's shadow. You have a right to express joy, disappointment, or the need for support.

For many, shame is the muzzle that keeps them silent. Some worry that if they express a boundary like, "Please don't raise your voice at me," people will see them as weak or oversensitive. But declaring a boundary isn't a weakness. It's saying, *"I value my peace and dignity enough not to let them be trampled."* When someone criticizes you for having needs, that reaction often says more about them than you. God never meant for you to live in silent discomfort to keep others comfortable.

In Scripture, we see examples of people who risked speaking up in brokenness. The woman with the issue of blood, for instance, approached Jesus publicly despite all social norms, screaming for her to remain hidden. She voiced her need—albeit by action—and found healing on the other side of her courage. In the same way, your healing journey includes learning to articulate your wounds, boundaries and wants. Silence only prolongs the lie that your needs don't matter.

If speaking your truth feels overwhelming, begin with something manageable. Maybe it's telling a friend, "I need a moment to gather my thoughts," instead of letting a conversation steamroll you. Or gently stating, "That comment hurt me," instead of pretending everything's fine. Each time you do this, you take a small sledgehammer to the walls, trauma built around your voice. Over time, the cracks become bigger, letting the light of authentic communication flood in.

Now, caution is needed when you begin to speak your truth with courage. Don't feel you must dive straight into a confrontational topic. If you seldom voice your needs, practice first with safer scenarios. Tell a coworker, "I'd prefer to meet in the afternoon—my morning is hectic." Notice how it feels to honor your own preference. Or, in your family, say, "I'd rather we talk about that tomorrow when I'm not so tired." You might be surprised at how many people respect what you communicate, especially when it's calm and clear. Each of these small victories reinforces the truth that your words are valuable.

Speaking your truth also means acknowledging your limits. If you've survived trauma, you might have spent years catering to others or enduring situations that trampled your sense of safety. Boundaries are the fences that protect what is sacred to you—your time, your emotional well-being, and your convictions. When you say, "I'm not comfortable discussing this right now," or "I need you to lower your voice," you are not being difficult; you're exercising self-care.

At first, setting boundaries can feel like stepping out onto a stage under a spotlight. You wonder if you'll be booed off or the crowd will mock you. But boundaries are more about how you respect yourself than how others respond. And if someone refuses to honor those boundaries, it reveals something about whether they truly value you as a person. Even Jesus withdrew from crowds when He needed rest, modeling that it's okay to say "enough" for now. Following that example reminds you that life doesn't have to be a continuous exposure to people's demands. You can carve out emotional and mental space to breathe.

Trauma might have taught you to hide parts of who you are. You may have concealed your sense of humor or strong opinions because blending into the background felt safer. Speaking your truth with courage means you allow yourself to shine without fear of rejection. It doesn't guarantee everyone will applaud your authenticity; some may be uncomfortable with the new, more confident you. But living authentically breaks the chains of self-doubt that trauma locks around your heart. You realize that what you have to say, how you feel, and who you are beneath the layers of coping deserve respect—first from yourself, then from those around you.

Communicating your truth is not about demanding attention. It's about refusing to let your soul fade under the weight of unspoken pains. When you speak, do it with grace, but do it firmly. You can say, "I feel afraid when you use that tone, and I need us to communicate differently," or "I love you, but I can't be your emotional dumping ground right now—I'm healing." These statements might prompt discomfort but also pave the road to clearer, healthier relationships.

Don't forget that God gave you this voice for a reason. Scripture shows us repeatedly that words have power—life, and death lie in the tongue. Imagine if you used your tongue to declare the truth about your situation: "I am worthy of love," "I deserve respectful treatment," and "My thoughts and feelings matter, too." Prayer is part of this. Before a challenging conversation, whisper, "Lord, guide my words. Help me speak with honesty and gentleness." Afterward, pray for peace in your spirit and for wisdom to handle any fallout. The point is to weave faith into your communication, recognizing that God cares about how you express your innermost self.

Also, consider that your voice can be an instrument of healing for others. There might be people in your circle—colleagues, friends, or even family members—who have struggles but never dared speak. They may be inspired to do likewise when they see you step forward, respectfully claiming your space in a conversation. In that way, speaking your truth doesn't just free you; it creates ripple effects of honesty and support in your community.

Speaking your truth with courage can feel exhilarating. But it can also leave you feeling raw and exposed, especially if you're not used to it. You might walk away from a conversation, second-guessing every word: "Did I say too much? Was I rude?" That's normal. Growth often comes with an aftertaste of vulnerability. But remember the bigger picture: each time you choose to be honest, you peel back a layer of hurt or isolation, stepping into a life where your voice, feelings, and experiences are not silenced by fear or shame.

Sometimes, the outcomes may be messy. People might react defensively. They might not immediately understand your new approach to communication. But don't let that deter you. Healing conversations often bloom in follow-up dialogues. You can clarify your intent: "I'm not blaming you; I just need to express how this impacts me." Over time, if they care about you, they'll learn to respect the boundaries and truths you share. And if they don't, that tells you something about the health of that relationship and whether it's a place you can safely invest yourself.

Like every other aspect of mending from trauma, reclaiming your voice is a process. Some days, you'll nail it, speaking assertively yet kindly. On other days, you may slip back into silent corners, weighed down by old fears. Give yourself grace. There's no master checklist for perfect communication, just daily opportunities to say, "I'm here; I have a perspective, and it deserves to be heard." With each small act of truthful speech, you stand a little taller, shedding shame and stepping deeper into self-respect.

Lastly, speaking your truth aligns you with the person God created you to be—someone not defined by old wounds but guided by honesty, integrity, and faith. As you continue walking this path, you'll find that courage grows in your chest like a tender shoot, breaking through the hard soil trauma once created. Keep nurturing it. Keep speaking with humility and boldness. Eventually, you'll see how a once-quiet voice can carry the weight of a healing testimony for yourself and those who still wait to speak their truth.

Reflection Questions

1. What truths about yourself have you been hesitant to speak aloud?

2. How can sharing your story become a tool for healing and connection?

3. What fears hold you back from speaking your truth, and how can you confront them?

4. In what spaces do you feel safe to express your authentic self?

5. How can courage in communication deepen your relationships?

CHAPTER 9

RECONNECTING WITH FAITH COMMUNITIES

P eople are messy. Because communities are made up of people, communities are messy as well. That being said, take a moment to recall the first time you felt truly accepted in a gathering of believers—maybe it was a small church group, a youth retreat, or a simple prayer group. You found yourself around people who didn't just smile politely but genuinely wanted to hear your story. Such moments can be powerful—even life-changing—especially when you're healing from old wounds and scars. But trauma can also turn communities into complex issues: you might feel cautious about walking into a church service or a small Bible study, worried that your story might be judged or dismissed.

But the truth is faith communities, when nurtured in love, can become a profound extension of God's healing touch. Think of them like rivers flowing with empathy and support, where your burdens are gently borne by many shoulders rather than just your own. By now, we have established that trauma often isolates you, making you feel that no one else can grasp the depth of your hurt. But when you encounter people who love and serve in Christ's name, you begin to realize you aren't alone—and that realization can be a game-changer for your healing journey.

We were never designed to walk this life by ourselves. From the beginning, Scripture reveals God's intention for us to live in fellowship and share each other's joys and sorrows. Faith communities can foster an environment where vulnerability isn't mocked but honored, where prayer isn't just a routine but a real encouragement that tangibly lifts your spirit. Picture this scenario: you come to a small group feeling a bit shaky—maybe you had a tough week reliving past trauma. You gather in a circle and share a fraction of your story. Instead of pity or impatience, you see understanding eyes and hear a chorus of voices saying, "We're praying with you." That collective support can make you feel like someone else is helping carry the weight on your heart for the first time.

Of course, not every faith gathering is a perfect haven. People are people. We all have flaws and shortcomings that we battle with. Like I said earlier, people are messy. But somewhere out there, there's a circle of believers genuinely yearning to love as Christ loves. And if you're patient and discerning enough to find that circle, the connection you build can be a cornerstone of your healing process.

Maybe you tried connecting before and found yourself hurt by gossip, judgment, or a lack of compassion. That pain can linger, making you hesitant to walk through church doors again or open up in another prayer group. Acknowledge that fear honestly: *"Lord, I'm scared of being hurt again."* Then, remember that one bad experience—or even several—doesn't nullify the existence of caring, empathetic communities. Even biblical heroes faced misunderstandings and hurt within spiritual circles. But they continued seeking genuine fellowship because it was essential to their growth.

Consider taking a small step: attending a low-pressure event, like a casual fellowship meal or an online faith-based meetup. Observe the culture. Do the people listen respectfully or dismiss concerns with quick clichés? Are they interested in each other's well-being, or is it all surface talk? As you see glimpses of genuine compassion, your trust can inch open, allowing you to engage further.

Every community has its personality—some are quiet and introspective, others lively and charismatic. There's no one-size-fits-all formula but look for three key signs: empathy, humility, and honesty. Empathy is important because trauma healing often needs hearts that can feel alongside you, not rush you. Humility, because a group that admits its own struggles creates space for you to share yours. Honesty is vital because healing thrives when masks come off, and people discuss their joys and battles.

Sometimes, you'll discover a small group dedicated to trauma survivors or folks navigating mental health challenges. Or a prayer circle at a local church that meets weekly to uplift personal requests. If you can't find something local, online communities like forums and virtual Bible studies can also be lifelines, offering connectivity and prayer support without geographical limits. The key is intention: choose a community that honors real-life issues, not just polished facades. You need a place where it's safe to be raw, to say, "I'm hurting today," and know that someone will kneel beside you in prayer rather than stare with condemnation.

In faith gatherings, you might feel pressured to share everything immediately—especially if the group culture is built on vulnerability. However, remember the power of pacing yourself. Trust grows over time. You can say, "I've gone through some difficult things in my past, and I'm slowly learning to heal," without unloading every detail if you're not ready. Let your heart lead you gradually. Over time, as you see how the community responds to smaller pieces of your story, you'll sense whether you can safely share more.

And if, after you share, you encounter compassion, tears of understanding, or honest prayers spoken on your behalf, that's a strong sign you're in a good place. If you encounter dismissal or judgment, it might indicate seeking another environment more aligned with the grace and empathy you need. Don't let one negative experience define every faith community. Keep searching. The Body of Christ is vast, and many pockets will rejoice to walk alongside you in sincere love.

As you reconnect, you might face the challenge of forgiving past hurts inflicted by church folks. Sometimes, the most challenging wounds come from those who claim to follow God. If you harbor bitterness or disappointment, give yourself permission to process it—pray, journal, or even talk to a counselor. Forgiveness doesn't mean ignoring the harm done but freeing yourself from the weight of resentment. By letting go of that baggage, you clear space to receive the blessings of a healthier faith community.

Your journey inspires others to address their own wounds from faith communities. Healing can ripple outward when you model that you were hurt, but God can still bring forth communities that nurture rather than harm. Your renewed faith in collective worship or study can sometimes re-ignite someone else's hope. They see you leaning into fellowship, scars and all and realize maybe they, too, can find solace in the arms of believers.

Worshiping together—whether through singing, reading Scripture, or group prayer—carries a unique healing balm. When you lift your voice among others, you're reminded that this journey isn't just you vs. the world. The harmony of voices speaks to a unity that transcends personal battles. In these moments, you can feel chains loosening, negative mindsets dissolving, and your spirit aligning with hope you didn't know you still had.

Even if you typically prefer quiet reflection, allow yourself to soak in corporate worship at times. There's power in hearing the Word preached in a loving environment, seeing heads bowed in mutual reverence, and sensing that the same God who meets you in your solitary prayers also meets you here, among His gathered children. Trauma tells you to isolate; worship reminds you that you belong.

Reconnecting with a faith community isn't a one-and-done milestone. You might try multiple groups or shift from one season's fellowship to another. You'll discover new relationships forming, each with the potential to reflect God's kindness into your healing journey. Commit to cultivating those bonds when you find a place that resonates with your spirit—one that feels safe, loving, and open. That might mean attending regularly, volunteering in small ways, or offering your story to encourage someone else.

Yes, it's vulnerable to lean into fellowship again, especially if trauma pushes you away from communal life. But vulnerability often becomes the birthplace of profound renewal. It is essential to realize that vulnerability is strength. Little by little, you learn that while we can fail, we can also uplift. While we all have flaws, we can also be conduits of grace. And in that mixture of our human imperfection and divine love, we find a belonging that nurtures the seeds of healing we've been tending on our own.

So gather your courage. Step back into the sanctuary, the Bible study, or the small group. Ask God to guide you to kindred souls who bear each other's burdens compassionately. Over time, you may see that faith communities, far from being an optional add-on, can be instruments of God's restoring power—places where your scars are understood, your tears are seen, and your testimonies of growth spark hope in everyone around you. May you walk into that fellowship with expectancy, ready to see your healing journey magnified by the warmth of shared faith and love.

Reflection Questions

1. How has your connection to faith communities influenced your healing journey?

2. What role does fellowship play in fostering emotional and spiritual growth?

3. What barriers prevent you from fully engaging in faith-based communities?

4. How can you contribute to creating spaces of healing and belonging for others?

5. In what ways can you reconnect with a sense of spiritual family?

CHAPTER 10

CELEBRATING PROGRESS

While speaking at a community event, I met a man named Marcus—tall, quiet, with eyes that told stories of battles fought in silence. During a break, he shared a piece of his story. "A few years ago," he said, "I hiked this tough mountain trail—I'd never done it before. Halfway up, I felt like I was done. My legs were shaking, and my heart was racing; I was sure I couldn't go any further. But then, an old hiker passing by stopped and said, "Don't fixate on the top of the mountain. Look behind you. See how far you've come." Marcus smiled, but there was weight to it. He continued, "I turned around, and there it was—the long winding path I'd already climbed. That was the moment I made it to the top." Then he paused and said, "Healing has been like that for me too."

Marcus' words stuck with me. Because that's what trauma does to us—it blinds us to what we've already done. We focus on the mountaintop, still to be conquered, and forget the many steps we've already taken. But healing isn't about getting to the top. It's about noticing the strength that's been growing with each step up. It's about recognizing and celebrating your progress in this journey.

Trauma can lock your attention on everything that still feels broken. You might be convinced there's too much left to mend, too many triggers left untested, too many memories that still sting. But if you don't also acknowledge the parts of you that have grown stronger, you risk losing heart before the journey's done. Celebrating your progress isn't arrogance or denial of what remains undone—it's the breath of fresh air your weary soul needs to keep climbing.

One of the simplest ways to affirm your growth is by noting your victories, no matter how small. Did you navigate a trigger slightly calmer than last time? Please write it down. Did you articulate a boundary without your voice trembling quite so much? Mark it. After a while, you'll have a record proving you're not stuck—you're evolving daily.

Don't underestimate the power of actually writing or typing these moments out. Our minds tend to forget the little triumphs, holding onto negative experiences like they're etched in stone. By recording your wins—whether in a journal or a note on your phone—you create tangible proof that healing is authentic, that your scars are indeed shifting from burdens to testimonies of survival.

For many who've survived trauma, self-acknowledgment can feel forbidden. You might have internalized messages like, "Don't be self-centered," or "Don't draw attention to yourself." Let me be clear, affirming that you're making progress isn't selfish; it's a way to steward the miracle of your own resilience. God delights in seeing His children grow, just as we delight in watching a seed sprout and blossom. If the Maker of the universe cherishes your steps, why wouldn't you?

This doesn't mean you become blind to areas needing more work. You can hold both realities: there's further to go, and you've already traveled a significant distance. When doubt creeps in, telling you you're not improving, you'll have a storehouse of recorded progress to counter that lie, reminding yourself that change is occurring.

It might sound trivial, but offering yourself a small token of reward can reinforce your transformation. That reward doesn't have to be elaborate—maybe it's enjoying a relaxing soak with essential oils, buying a new journal or a bouquet of fresh flowers, or scheduling a quiet afternoon to read a favorite book. The point is that highlighting your progress is a good thing, and it's worth honoring.

Some people worry that rewarding themselves is frivolous. But consider how scripture often called for celebration after a victory or a significant milestone—feasts, songs, or memorial stones. Those celebrations helped the community remember God's faithfulness. In your case, a simple gesture of self-care can become a modern version of marking the moment, telling your heart, *"We did it—look how far God has brought us."*

The next step after noticing growth is usually letting trusted people celebrate with you. Maybe you quietly confide to a friend, "I went a whole day without being overwhelmed by that trigger," or, "I actually told someone 'no' without feeling crushed by guilt." Their cheers or encouraging words can amplify your sense of accomplishment. There's a mysterious power in having someone else acknowledge your growth; it's as though the progress becomes more real when witnessed by another.

Even in faith communities, telling your story of small victories can uplift everyone. People often think testimonies have to be grand or miraculous. But there's beauty in testifying, "I felt calmer when an argument started at work," or, "I noticed my body tensed less this week." Others may be inspired, and you'll feel that resonance of shared hope—a sense that, in God's design, all steps forward deserve a spotlight, however slight they may seem.

Keep in mind that every step forward is also an act of worship. God isn't just passively watching your healing; He's actively involved, providing strength and wisdom you can't muster alone. Therefore, celebrating progress can become a moment of praise. *"Thank You, Lord, for giving me courage today. Thank You for guiding me past that fear."* Such gratitude keeps your eyes open to divine involvement, reminding you that you're not the sole architect of your mending but a co-laborer with grace itself.

Don't miss the chance to turn your progress into a testimony that lifts someone else's burden. You never know who's sitting quietly, convinced they'll never overcome their triggers or silence their anxious thoughts.

Your story of small steps—how you managed to reduce a panic episode from an hour to fifteen minutes, or how you spoke your boundaries for the first time—might be the ray of light they need to keep going.

Sometimes, the best ministry isn't a polished sermon but a heartfelt, *"I've been there, and I see how far you can come."* When you open up about your progress—moving from near-despair to a sense of possibility—you become living proof that healing doesn't always burst forth in dramatic leaps. Often, it's a gentle unfolding, a day-to-day process that can still yield astounding outcomes.

Let's be honest: progress isn't a perfect straight line. You'll have days—or weeks—where it feels like you've lost ground. Maybe a surge of anxiety returns unexpectedly, or an old memory triggers fresh tears. Such setbacks can cast a shadow over your mind, making you question if any progress is real. This is why celebrating wins is crucial: once you've established the habit of acknowledging growth, you won't be so quick to believe the setback means starting from zero.

Setbacks can also be instructive. They spotlight areas that still need attention or reveal triggers you hadn't fully addressed. Rather than viewing these moments as proof of failure, see them as opportunities to refine your coping strategies and reaffirm your resilience. After all, you've already proven you can grow—your records and progress confirm it—so a stumble shouldn't derail your entire journey.

As you complete each chapter of your healing, pause at that metaphorical mountaintop, even if it's just a brief landing. Reflect on the distance traveled and the muscles you've developed—both emotional and spiritual. Take a moment to breathe in the wonder that you're not who you were a month or a year ago. And then, after soaking in that moment of celebration, fix your gaze forward again. The path continues. New layers of freedom await. But you'll walk it differently, guided by the evidence of your own progress.

Remember, trauma once shrank your vision down to a narrow corridor of pain, but these celebrations widen your scope. They remind you that you're resilient and that there is room in your story for laughter, growth, and deeper trust in God's redeeming power. Each celebration is a foothold you secure on the mountain, ensuring you won't fall back into despair without a fight. The climb is ongoing, but the vantage point keeps getting brighter.

So celebrate. Dance if you want, cry tears of relief, whisper gratitude under your breath, or enjoy a quiet cup of tea under the open sky. Let your heart say, "I've come this far, and by God's grace, I'll keep going." In that simple act, you honor your journey, your Creator, and the promise of wholeness you're steadily embracing. It might not solve every issue overnight, but it will affirm that your efforts have a tangible impact—and that, my friend, is a powerful fuel for the future.

Reflection Questions

1. How do you define progress in your healing journey, and what milestones have you reached?

2. Why is it important to celebrate small victories along the way?

3. What practices help you acknowledge growth while still being patient with setbacks?

4. How can you honor your resilience while continuing to pursue deeper healing?

5. What routines or traditions can you create to mark moments of progress?

CHAPTER 11

HANDLING SETBACKS WITH PATIENCE

"How could I have allowed this to happen? I thought I was past this." Ever whispered those words after an unexpected breakdown? After a panic, you didn't see coming? After anger flared in a way you swore you've outgrown? There's something brutal about setbacks. It's like reaching the top of a staircase only to tumble back down many steps. The bruises sting more, not because the fall was worse, but because *you thought you were further along*. And that sting? It's not just pain. It's shame. The voice sneers at you, *"You should be over this by now."*

But here's what no one tells you: growth is messy. Growth is unpredictable. It loops. It doubles back before it leaps forward. And sometimes, the stumble is part of the design. Because healing isn't about never falling again—it's about how you rise differently each time.

Setbacks can be disheartening, especially if you believe you've finally closed the door on certain scars. So, go easy on yourself. Give yourself grace because this healing journey is about recognizing that each time you fall, you're allowed to stand back up. Handling setbacks with patience starts by telling yourself the truth: *"Yes, I fell, but this fall does not erase the ground I've gained."* Trauma is persistent, but so is the grace that undergirds your every step. In fact, the Bible tells us that God has given us more grace than the stuff that we are dealing with, which means our trauma will never outrun our grace. You might limp momentarily, catching your breath from the blow, but you won't lose the opportunity to reach your destination.

Traumatic memories can be sneaky, nestled in your body and mind like buried seeds waiting for the right conditions to sprout. Maybe a particular smell, a long-forgotten photo, or a stressful situation triggers a reaction you thought you'd outgrown. It's frustrating. You've practiced grounding, rewritten negative thoughts, and found glimpses of joy, but suddenly, that old panic or pain has returned.

Often, setbacks occur because healing isn't a linear, single-file line. Think of it more like a spiral, where each turn brings you closer to wholeness. However, you might still circle past familiar emotional terrain. You see the same landscape from a slightly higher vantage point, even if it looks painfully similar. If you remind yourself that each setback is part of the curve—part of the process—you avoid jumping to the conclusion that all is lost.

When a setback hits, the crucial question is: *How do I respond now, compared to before?* Maybe you still feel anxious but notice you're more aware. You reach for grounding techniques or whisper a prayer instead of letting fear overpower you. Perhaps you still experience flashbacks, but you bounce back quicker, or maybe you're now able to call a friend or seek comfort in Scripture rather than sink into a week-long trap of despair. These shifts, however subtle, prove that you have changed. See, setbacks don't negate your growth; they test it.

If, at first, you respond in old ways, give yourself time. However, if you realize you're spiraling, you will need to apply new coping tools. You also need to recognize that this realization proves you're making progress. In the past, you might have been stuck in that spiral for a month. Now, it might only be days or hours before you get out of it. Don't let shame tell you that a slip-up means you've failed. Call it what it is: a stumble on the path because the truth is it's not a reversal of the entire road you've already walked.

One blessing of coming this far is that you likely have a better support system: a counselor, a trusted friend, or a faith community that prays with you. When you face a setback, it's time to lean on them, not withdraw from them. Trauma will say, *"You're too much trouble. Don't bother them with this old issue."* Understand that experiencing a setback is when you need someone to speak the truth about your fears, remind you of your progress, and stand beside you in prayer.

Reaching out takes vulnerability, humility, and courage. You might be afraid that people will be disappointed or think you haven't been trying hard enough. However, genuine support circles understand that healing is rarely a straight line. They'll rejoice that you're still in the fight, that you're not letting the enemy of your soul keep you isolated in silence. If you find a community that can celebrate small wins, they can undoubtedly help support you in a setback.

Setbacks can feel cruel, but they can also offer insight. Perhaps this stumble reveals you still have an unhealed corner of your heart—an event you never entirely processed, a boundary you never firmly established. The pain might point you to the next layer of work you need to do. You move from surface-level healing to deeper restoration by identifying these hidden triggers and unresolved hurts.

Invite God into that discovery process. Ask in prayer, *"Lord, what is this setback showing me? What do I still need to release, forgive, or adjust?"* With each honest question, you open a door for God's guidance. He may prompt you to revisit a specific memory in therapy, to have a clarifying conversation with a mentor, or to forgive someone you still hold anger toward. While revisiting old wounds is never pleasant, it's often the path to our greatest freedom.

Scripture portrays many characters who experienced moments of triumph followed by sudden lapses. Elijah went from a miraculous victory on Mount Carmel to fleeing in fear and despair. Peter boldly declared faith one day, then denied Jesus under pressure the next. The common thread in these stories is that God's grace remained steadfast. He met them in their low points, restoring and reminding them of their calling. Your setbacks don't chase away the God who's walked with you this far. He's still there, ready to anchor you if you let Him.

In practical terms, re-center on God's promises whenever a setback arises. You might read a favorite psalm or play, on repeat, a worship song that helps you sense His closeness. It doesn't have to be lengthy—sometimes a simple prayer like, *"Lord, I feel shaken, but I know You are unshakable,"* can steady your spirit. The more quickly you reconnect with the truth of His presence, the less power the setback has to spin you back into hopelessness.

Let's say you had a panic attack yesterday, your first in months. The old voice scolds, *"See, you haven't changed."* But pause. Reflect. Did you stay in that panic as long as before? Did you use a grounding technique that helped reduce its intensity? Did you reach out for help more promptly? Those might seem like small consolations but are tangible signs of growth. Even setbacks can highlight how differently you now respond to stress. The new you is revealed in how you pick yourself up, how you dust yourself off, and how you refuse to let one event define the entirety of your progress.

Patience is a companion you must welcome in this journey—patience with your mind, emotions, and body. Patience helps you keep your eyes on the bigger picture. You are not who you were at the start of this journey. The fruit of your efforts—the calmer mornings, the softer self-talk, the renewed boundaries—testify that progress is real. Setbacks are temporary disruptions on a road that still leads forward. *"I press on,"* the apostle Paul wrote, acknowledging he hadn't arrived yet but was committed to pushing ahead. Embrace that same mindset, trusting God's hand to hold you through every stumble.

Most of all, speak kindly to yourself when you fall. Say, *"Yes, this hurts. Yes, I'm disappointed. But I'm still here, learning and anchored in God's grace."* That posture of self-compassion shields you from the crippling effects of shame. Then, use your toolkit—grounding exercises, supportive relationships, faith-based affirmations—and use them wholeheartedly, and continue climbing. The destination is still ahead, and every step matters, even the ones that momentarily cause you to pause and evaluate where you're at on this journey.

As time passes, you'll look back on these setbacks as chapters in your story that strengthened your determination. They forced you to effectively readjust your coping strategies, reaffirm your identity in Christ, and trust the community around you. They showed you that a moment of falling doesn't define your entire path. So keep pressing on with a patience that honors your humanity and the God who never gives up on you.

As you rise from each stumble, resilience takes a deeper root in your soul. Trauma might have intended to keep you bound, but each setback faced with faith becomes evidence that darkness cannot hold back a spirit bent on healing. Let that sink in: *darkness cannot hold back a spirit bent on healing.* That's your story now—a story where you handle setbacks with patience, anchored in the unending faithfulness of God, continually moving closer to the wholeness you were destined to claim.

Reflection Questions

1. How do you typically respond to setbacks, and what shifts could help you approach them with patience?

2. What self-compassion practices can you use when facing moments of frustration or disappointment?

3. How can setbacks become opportunities for reflection and deeper growth?

4. What spiritual truths remind you that healing is not linear?

5. How can you hold onto hope during seasons of slow progress?

CHAPTER 12

EMBRACING A LIFE OF CONTINUED GROWTH

S ome people imagine healing as a single destination—a point on the map labeled "fully recovered," where trauma never again casts a shadow. Real healing seldom works that way. It's more like discovering a winding trail that continues long after the scenery changes. Each turn brings new challenges and fresh victories. You probably started this journey feeling weighed down by wounds from the past. Over time, you've learned essential daily practices, nurtured faith's steady help, and faced old anxieties with fresh courage. Congratulations, you're making progress. Nonetheless, it's time you embrace the truth: your life of growth and healing doesn't end here. In fact, you're still at the beginning.

But before you look to the future, pause and reflect on the ground you've covered. Think back to the first days of confronting your trauma—those uncertain steps, the hesitance to trust yourself and others. Take time and appreciate how you stand a little taller. Maybe your shoulders aren't permanently pinned to your ears. Perhaps you speak up more readily when something feels off or find it easier to breathe through moments that used to send you spiraling. Yes, you still have struggles, but you're not the same person you once were.

Give yourself permission to celebrate that transformation. Too often, we hurry on to the next hurdle without honoring the perseverance it took to arrive here. Each chapter you've traversed deserves a moment of gratitude. Write it down in a journal, share it in a small group, or spend a quiet moment with God, whispering thanks for progress that once felt impossible.

Growth is never meant to be stagnant. When you prune a plant, you do so not to stifle it but to help it flourish even more. The same principle applies to your emotional and spiritual life. After gaining these new tools and perspectives, you may desire to explore other areas that once felt off-limits, like volunteering at a community center, mentoring someone just starting their healing journey, or pursuing a dream you shelved long ago.

Embracing a life of continued growth means giving yourself the freedom to keep discovering. Trauma told you to stay in a small, guarded corner. But as you mend, you realize the world is bigger, and your part in it can be braver. You don't have to remain confined to who you were in your darkest season; you can venture into unfamiliar opportunities, trusting that the faith and resilience you've developed can guide you forward.

You've seen how faith can serve as a solid anchor by now. But this isn't the time to settle into a minimal prayer routine or an occasional Scripture verse. Consider how you might deepen your walk with God now that you have tasted the power of His presence in your healing process. Perhaps you schedule longer periods of reflection or study a passage of Scripture with an eye for how it speaks to the layers of your journey. Maybe you can join a prayer team or a faith-based workshop that will challenge you to grow in areas beyond trauma recovery.

Like any relationship, your connection with God thrives on consistent engagement. If you had a close friend who guided you through a rough patch, wouldn't you want to keep that friendship flourishing even after the crisis? In the same way, keep nurturing your relationship with God. He was with you when the nights were darkest, and He rejoices as He sees you step into brighter days. Deepening your spiritual disciplines secures your foundation, ensuring that as life brings fresh turns, you remain grounded in divine love rather than old fears.

One of the miracles of mending is that you begin to see beyond your own pain. Your scars become empathy for those who are still in the thick of their struggle. So many people wander through life convinced no one can understand their hidden wounds. But you do. You've walked that valley, and you carry the stories of what it took to climb out. Sharing that testimony can shine a beacon of hope for someone trapped.

This doesn't mean you must become a professional counselor—unless that's your calling. Sometimes, just listening to someone's story without judgment, offering a comforting word, or pointing them to practical resources is enough to spark transformation. It's a quiet ministry, but it resonates powerfully because you're offering what you once so desperately needed: acceptance and guidance without condemnation. By helping others, you reinforce your own growth, realizing that all you endured can be turned around for good and used by God to heal the hearts of those who are hurting.

A life of continued growth doesn't mean you'll never face new traumas or emotional storms. We live in a world where unexpected hurts can still blindside us. The difference is now you're equipped with a deeper trust in God's sustaining power, plus the practical habits that help you process the emotions that trauma used to restrict you. When you encounter fresh challenges—an illness, a job setback, or a strained relationship—you can lean on the same grounding, self-compassion, boundary-setting, and faith-based methods you've been developing.

At first, you might feel old anxieties flaring up. Don't panic. Remind yourself, *"I've gained the ability to handle this step by step."* You now know how to breathe through tension. You know how to speak your truth when needed. You know how to reach out to community or professional help before a crisis engulfs you. And you know that God stands as an unwavering constant, whether you're rejoicing on a mountaintop or trudging through a valley. This confidence in your resilience and in God's support becomes a lifeline in every future trial.

As you close this chapter of active healing, keep your gaze forward. Healing, you've learned, is a lifelong evolution, not a one-time fix. That can sound discouraging, but in truth, it's liberating. There's always more life to explore, more aspects of your heart to discover, and more testimonies to share. You may need to revisit some coping tools periodically or refresh your perspective when triggers resurface. But each time, you approach them with greater understanding, having laid down solid groundwork in these mending days.

Finally, don't lose sight of gratitude. Look back with thankfulness at how far you've come, acknowledging that, yes, you did the hard work, but God's grace and maybe even some supportive folks along the way helped you push through. You might consider writing a short gratitude list, naming specific moments or people who played a role in your transformation. Let that gratitude shape your hope for tomorrow. If you were carried this far, there's no telling what further joys and victories await as you grow.

Embracing a life of continued growth is the grand invitation at the heart of your healing journey. It bids you farewell from the darkest pages, ushering you into a narrative marked by resilience, compassion, and faith. The scars may remain, but they no longer dictate your story. Instead, they stand as reminders of how a spirit, anchored in God's love, can heal and thrive. My friend, go forward with courage because the One who began a good work in you will see you through into a radiant next season and beyond. A season where you can truly bloom.

Reflection Questions

1. What does a life of continued growth look like for you beyond the healing process?

2. How can you cultivate habits that sustain emotional and spiritual well-being long-term?

3. What role does ongoing learning play in your journey of restoration?

4. How can you use your healing story to empower and uplift others?

5. In what ways can you remain open to new growth even in seasons of stability?

Epilogue

After all the twists and turns you've walked through in these pages, a hush settles over your spirit, a gentle exhale. You've navigated triggers and tension, confronted hidden shame, learned to rest your soul in still moments, and dared to trust people and possibilities again. This process called for more than mental resolve; it demanded faith in a loving God who removes from the mess and small daily steps that rewrite your relationship with fear. And now, standing at the close of *Mended*, you're no longer the same person who started.

Think of it like surveying a house you've spent months renovating. The external walls are still familiar, but the inside feels renewed. Yes, some rooms might still need a little work—corners waiting to be painted or re-organized. But the foundation is stronger, and the living spaces are more welcoming. In the same way, you've taken your life's blueprint—once marked by trauma—and begun to shape it into a dwelling of hope. Each new habit, each boundary, each prayerful pause is another beam, another nail, another fresh coat of paint.

But remember, *Mended* doesn't claim to be the final word on your healing. It's a step—a sacred milestone on a continuing path. You'll still
face days when old aches surface. There'll be moments you wonder if
you've regressed. Yet the difference now is that you're equipped with
practical strategies and a deeper awareness of God's presence in every
breath. You no longer have to stumble in the dark; you have the light of
daily faith rhythms, supportive community, and your own blossoming
self-knowledge guiding you forward.

Carry these lessons with you. Keep grounding yourself when panic
threatens. Keep rewriting harmful thoughts with Scripture-based truth.
Keep claiming your right to boundaries and honest communication.
Keep honoring your body with gentle movement and your heart with
moments of stillness. Above all, keep welcoming God into each sunrise
and sunset. Invite Him to shine over your small triumphs and big leaps
of faith.

If you look back at times, uncertain about the distance left to travel, pause
and celebrate just how far you've come. Celebrate the pockets of peace
that once felt impossible. Celebrate the relationships that have grown
more authentic and the silent burdens you've shared and lightened.
These are real victories, testaments to the resilience God planted in you.

And now you stand on the brink of a future that's not defined by your
wounds but by your ongoing healing. Each day is an opportunity to
build upon the foundation you've laid here: stepping out of survival
mode and into the fullness of a life shaped by calm mornings, stable
hearts, grounded faith, and a willingness to keep growing. Let that vi-

sion inspire you to keep walking, believing that even greater peace and purpose await.

Thank you for bringing your heart to this journey. May you open the door to tomorrow with gentle confidence, fully mended in some places, still in progress in others, but wholly supported by a God who has never left your side. Let hope define your next steps, dear friend. In the tenderness of His grace and the strength of your resolve, you are indeed *Mended*—body, soul, and spirit—and ready to continue toward ever-growing wholeness.

What's Next

You've journeyed through *Mended*, discovering the daily routines and faith-infused habits that anchor your emotional well-being. You've seen how small, intentional practices—like a structured morning prayer or a midday pause—can bring together a network of stability you once thought impossible. Now you stand at another turning point, your heart steadied, your mind less captive to old triggers. So, *what next?*

In **The Trauma Detox** series, *Bloom* is what's next. *Bloom* represents the final phase. If *Scarred* revealed your wounds and *Mended* helped you heal them day by day. Then, *Bloom* invites you to thrive in ways you never imagined—discovering fresh purpose, deeper joy, and the chance to share your testimony with others. Where *Mended* was about reestablishing your footing, *Bloom* is about spreading your wings, letting your experiences fuel new adventures and service.

Before you rush forward, take a moment to honor the ground you've already covered. Look at the difference in how you handle conflict or how your body responds to stressful events. Reflect on the boundaries you learned to set or the triggers that once paralyzed you but now merely paused you. This progress deserves recognition. Give thanks to God for every subtle victory, for each day you felt a bit more like yourself.

As you prepare to enter *Bloom*, bring along the tools that served you well in *Mended*. Don't abandon the routines just because you feel stronger. In fact, those routines will support you as you reach for more, guiding you to new experiences with a secure safety net beneath. Also, remember that healing is an evolving journey. Some triggers might return, or new emotional challenges might surface. But you're equipped to face them with the resilience and faith you've developed here.

Let your next chapter be colored by expectancy. If *Mended* showed you how to stand without wobbling, *Bloom* will show you how to walk, run, and even soar. The seeds of self-compassion and spiritual discipline you planted can now bear fruit in the form of leadership, creativity, or heartfelt ministry. Keep your mind open, your spirit prayerful, and your heart tuned to opportunities God may bring your way. The horizon brims with promise.

So close this book not as an end but as a hinge that opens wide to a new dimension of life. You've done the diligent work of daily healing, proving that with faith and practice, trauma need not define your every moment. Now, in *Bloom*, you'll see how far your branches can extend, how radiant your bloom can truly become, and how your journey can inspire others to believe in second chances and persistent grace. May you step forward confidently, knowing that each day of consistent mending has prepared you for a bright future filled with undiscovered possibilities.

THE END